For:

Jared Jr.

From:

Gram Grace & Jim

Date:

Christmas 2011

Published in Nashville, Tennessee, by Tommy Nelson. Tommy Nelson is a
registered trademark of Thomas Nelson, Inc.

Scripture quotations are from the International Children's Bible®. © 1986, 1988,
1999 by Thomas Nelson, Inc. and the Reader Friendly Edition™, © 2009 by
Thomas Nelson, Inc. All rights reserved.

Thomas Nelson, Inc., titles may be purchased in bulk for educational, business,
fund-raising, or sales promotional use. For information, please e-mail
SpecialMarkets@ThomasNelson.com.

Library of Congress Cataloging-in-Publication Data

Bible. English. International Children's Bible. Selections. 2010.
God's promises for boys / [compiled by] Jack Countryman and [poetry by] Amy
Parker ; illustrations by Richard Watson.
    p. cm.
ISBN 978-1-4003-1592-5 (hardback)
1. Bible—Indexes—Juvenile. 2. Bible—Quotations—Juvenile. 3. Boys—Religious
life. 4. Christian children—Religious life. I. Countryman, Jack. II. Parker, Amy,
1976– III. Title.
BS432.B445 2010b
220.5'208—dc22   2009049197

Mfg. by Lake Book / Melrose Park, IL / November 2010 / PO # 115011

God's promises® for boys

jack countryman & amy parker

Illustrations by Richard Watson

A Division of Thomas Nelson Publishers

NASHVILLE   DALLAS   MEXICO CITY   RIO DE JANEIRO

Contents

God Wants You To . . .

You Want to Be Cool

Stylin', chillin', and rollin' your way
Are fine when you're breaking no rules.
But helpin', respectin', and followin' God's ways
Are the *only* way to be coooool.

Do not be shaped by this world. Instead be
changed within by a new way of thinking. Then you
will be able to decide what God wants for you.
And you will be able to know what is good and
pleasing to God and what is perfect.

ROMANS 12:2

. . .

So through Jesus let us always offer our sacrifice to
God. This sacrifice is our praise, coming from lips that
speak his name. Do not forget to do good to others.
And share with them what you have. These are
the sacrifices that please God.

HEBREWS 13:15–16

But you are chosen people. You are the King's priests.
You are a holy nation. You are a nation that belongs
to God alone. God chose you to tell about the
wonderful things he has done. He called you out
of darkness into his wonderful light.

1 PETER 2:9

You Are Happy

Hooray! It's a wonderful day!
Gone fishin' with bugs in a jar . . .
There's always a reason to be happy—
No matter *who* or *where* you are!

Ask and you will receive. And your joy
will be the fullest joy.

JOHN 16:24

• • •

You have not seen Christ, but still you love him.
You cannot see him now, but you believe in him.
You are filled with a joy that cannot be explained.
And that joy is full of glory.

1 PETER 1:8

• • •

The Lord has done great things for us,
and we are very glad.

PSALM 126:3

The Lord makes me very happy.
All that I am rejoices in my God.
The Lord has covered me with clothes of salvation.
He has covered me with a coat of goodness.

ISAIAH 61:10

You Are Thankful

For parents and friends who love you so much,
For trees to climb and warm sunlight,
For having *all* that you need—and more,
Say, "Thank You, God!" with all your might.

Thanks be to God for his gift that is
too wonderful to explain.

2 CORINTHIANS 9:15

. . .

Thank the Lord because he is good.
His love continues forever.

1 CHRONICLES 16:34

. . .

The Lord is my strength and shield.
I trust him, and he helps me.
I am very happy.
And I praise him with my song.

PSALM 28:7

Come, let's bow down and worship him.
Let's kneel before the Lord who made us.
He is our God.
And we are the people he takes care of
and the sheep that he tends.

PSALM 95:6—7

You Are Worried

Young soldier, don't you worry;
My son, don't you fret!
God hasn't met *any* problem
That's been too big for Him yet!

Give your worries to the Lord.
He will take care of you.

PSALM 55:22

• • •

You, Lord, give true peace.
You give peace to those who depend on you.
You give peace to those who trust you.
So, trust the Lord always.
Trust the Lord because he is our Rock forever.

ISAIAH 26:3–4

"I leave you peace. My peace I give you. I do not give it to you as the world does. So don't let your hearts be troubled. Don't be afraid."

JOHN 14:27

You Need Help

Searching for help? Nowhere to turn?
You've looked both high and low?
There's just one thing to remember:
Prayer is the best place to go.

People, trust God all the time.
Tell him all your problems. God is our protection.

PSALM 62:8

. . .

Trust the Lord with all your heart.
Don't depend on your own understanding.
Remember the Lord in everything you do.
And he will give you success.

PROVERBS 3:5—6

. . .

So our hope is in the Lord. He is our help,
our shield to protect us.

PSALM 33:20

God is our protection and our strength.
He always helps in times of trouble.
So we will not be afraid if the earth shakes,
or if the mountains fall into the sea.

PSALM 46:1–2

You Feel Guilty

A baseball dented the hood of Dad's car,
And everyone's looking at you. . . .
Just stop where you are and say, "I'm sorry."
It's the most important thing you can do.

"God did not send his Son into the world to judge the
world guilty, but to save the world through him. He
who believes in God's Son is not judged guilty."

JOHN 3:17–18

. . .

If anyone belongs to Christ, then he is made new.
The old things have gone; everything is made new!

2 CORINTHIANS 5:17

. . .

"I tell you the truth. Whoever hears what I say and
believes in the One who sent me has eternal life.
He will not be judged guilty. He has already left
death and has entered into life."

JOHN 5:24

"Don't judge other people, and you will not be judged. Don't accuse others of being guilty, and you will not be accused of being guilty. Forgive other people, and you will be forgiven."

LUKE 6:37

You Are Tempted to Do the Wrong Thing

The smell of fresh cookies fills the air,
But you remember Mom saying, "Don't!"
So when a sneaky voice says, "Yes, you *can*,"
Make sure your reply is, "I won't!"

[Y]ou can trust God. He will not let you be tempted more than you can stand. But when you are tempted, God will also give you a way to escape that temptation. Then you will be able to stand it.

1 CORINTHIANS 10:13

• • •

Control yourselves and be careful! The devil is your enemy. And he goes around like a roaring lion looking for someone to eat. Refuse to give in to the devil. Stand strong in your faith.

1 PETER 5:8–9

For this reason Jesus had to be made like his brothers in every way. . . . And now he can help those who are tempted. He is able to help because he himself suffered and was tempted.

HEBREWS 2:17–18

You Need to Be a Good Sport

The referee blew his whistle in your face,
And the other team just stole the ball. . . .
Yet making sure you have a good attitude
Is the winning-est rule of them all.

This is my prayer for you: that your love will grow
more and more; that you will have knowledge and
understanding with your love; that you will see the
difference between good and bad and choose the good; that
you will be pure and without wrong for the coming of
Christ; that you will be filled with the good things produced
in your life by Christ to bring glory and praise to God.

PHILIPPIANS 1:9—11

• • •

You should do good deeds to be an example in every
way for young men. . . . That is the way we should
live, because God's grace has come. That grace
can save every person.

TITUS 2:7, 11

Dear friends, we should love each other, because love comes from God. The person who loves has become God's child and knows God. Whoever does not love does not know God, because God is love.

1 JOHN 4:7–8

You Need Comfort

When your very best friend moves far away
Or your dog is nowhere to be found,
Turn to God, and you will find
His comforting love all around.

Praise be to the God and Father of our Lord Jesus
Christ. God is the Father who is full of mercy. And he
is the God of all comfort. He comforts us every time
we have trouble, so that we can comfort others when
they have trouble. We can comfort them with the
same comfort that God gives us.

2 CORINTHIANS 1:3–4

• • •

The Lord says, "I am the one who comforts you."

ISAIAH 51:12

• • •

God comforts those who are troubled.

2 CORINTHIANS 7:6

Jesus said, "Don't let your hearts be troubled.
Trust in God. And trust in me."

JOHN 14:1

You Need Forgiveness

After you've said, "I'm sorry,"
God will take care of the rest.
He'll forget about those bad things you've done
And only remember the best!

He has not punished us as our sins should be punished.
He has not repaid us for the evil we have done. . . .
He has taken our sins away from us
as far as the east is from west.

PSALM 103:10, 12

. . .

If we confess our sins, he will forgive our sins.

1 JOHN 1:9

. . .

Happy is the person whose sins are forgiven,
whose wrongs are pardoned.

PSALM 32:1

The Lord forgives me for all my sins.
He heals all my diseases.
He saves my life from the grave.
He loads me with love and mercy.

PSALM 103:3–4

You Are Angry

Did that boy in your class tattle on you?
Did your sister crash your go-cart?
Don't yell; don't pout; don't go around mad;
Ask God to put peace in your heart.

Do not be angry easily. Anger will not help you live a good life as God wants. So put out of your life every evil thing and every kind of wrong you do. Don't be proud but accept God's teaching that is planted in your hearts. This teaching can save your souls.

JAMES 1:19–21

• • •

Do not be angry with each other, but forgive each other. If someone does wrong to you, then forgive him. Forgive each other because the Lord forgave you.

COLOSSIANS 3:13

A gentle answer will calm a person's anger.
But an unkind answer will cause more anger.

PROVERBS 15:1

You Feel Lonely

Feeling left out and a little sad?
Stuck in the lonely zone?
Go to the One who is *always* there,
And you'll never be alone.

"So don't worry, because I am with you.
Don't be afraid, because I am your God.
I will make you strong and will help you.
I will support you with my right hand that saves you."

ISAIAH 41:10

• • •

"The mountains may disappear,
and the hills may come to an end.
But my love will never disappear.
My promise of peace will not come to an end,"
says the Lord who shows mercy to you.

ISAIAH 54:10

"I am with you and will save you," says the Lord.

JEREMIAH 30:11

• • •

"You can be sure that I will be with you always. I will
continue with you until the end of the world."

MATTHEW 28:20

You Want Your Own Way

So you didn't get to be shortstop,
Or play the game you wanted to play—
Keep your cool and remember this rule:
Make sure *your* way is God's way!

A wise person is careful and stays out of trouble.
But a foolish person is quick to act and careless.
A person who quickly loses his temper
does foolish things.
But a person with understanding remains calm.

PROVERBS 14:16–17

• • •

Yes, God is working in you to help you want
to do what pleases him. Then he gives you
the power to do it.

PHILIPPIANS 2:13

Help me obey your commands
because that makes me happy.
Help me want to obey your rules
instead of selfishly wanting riches.

PSALM 119:35–36

You Are Afraid

Monsters. Spiders. Being alone.
Do these things make you tremble in fear?
When you're afraid, remember these words:
God is with you; He's always near!

God did not give us a spirit that makes us afraid. He
gave us a spirit of power and love and self-control.

2 TIMOTHY 1:7

• • •

The Spirit that we received is not a spirit that makes
us slaves again to fear. The Spirit that we have
makes us children of God. And with that Spirit we say,
"Father, dear Father." And the Spirit himself joins
with our spirits to say that we are God's children.
If we are God's children, then we will receive
the blessings God has for us.

ROMANS 8:15–17

Where God's love is, there is no fear, because
God's perfect love takes away fear.

1 JOHN 4:18

. . .

I will not be afraid because the Lord is with me.
People can't do anything to me.

PSALM 118:6

The Man You'll Grow Up to Be

Go for it! Follow your dreams!
And whatever you seek to do—
Doctor, fireman, chief of police—
Follow the purpose God has for you!

"I am the true vine; my Father is the gardener. . . .
Remain in me, and I will remain in you. No branch
can produce fruit alone. It must remain in the vine. It
is the same with you. You cannot produce fruit alone.
You must remain in me."

JOHN 15:1, 4

• • •

God has chosen you and made you his holy people. He
loves you. So always do these things: Show mercy to
others; be kind, humble, gentle, and patient.

COLOSSIANS 3:12

Loving God means obeying his commands.
And God's commands are not too hard for us.
Everyone who is a child of God has the power to win
against the world. It is our faith that wins the victory
against the world. So the one who conquers the world is
the person who believes that Jesus is the Son of God.

1 JOHN 5:3–5

God's Love

Is God's love deep in your heart?
It's time to let it show!
Share a smile! Lend a hand!
Let it overflow!

This is how God showed his love to us: He sent his only
Son into the world to give us life through him. True
love is God's love for us, not our love for God. God
sent his Son to die in our place to take away our sins.

1 JOHN 4:9–10

• • •

And this hope will never disappoint us, because
God has poured out his love to fill our hearts. God
gave us his love through the Holy Spirit,
whom God has given to us.

ROMANS 5:5

But dear friends, use your most holy faith to build yourselves up strong. Pray with the Holy Spirit. Keep yourselves in God's love. Wait for the Lord Jesus Christ with his mercy to give you life forever.

JUDE 20–21

God's Grace

It's a second chance when you mess up,
Or God going easy when He could be tough.
But when you ask, He always forgives;
Yes, God's grace is more than enough.

And before the world was made, God decided to
make us his own children through Jesus Christ.
That was what he wanted and what pleased him.
This brings praise to God because of his wonderful
grace. God gave that grace to us freely, in Christ,
the One he loves. In Christ we are set free by the
blood of his death. And so we have forgiveness
of sins because of God's rich grace.

EPHESIANS 1:5—7

· · ·

The Lord God is like our sun and shield.
The Lord gives us kindness and glory.
He does not hold back anything good
from those whose life is innocent.

PSALM 84:11

The Word was full of grace and truth. From him we
all received more and more blessings.

JOHN 1:16

· • ·

But the Lord said to me, "My grace is enough for you.
When you are weak, then my power is made perfect in you."

2 CORINTHIANS 12:9

God's Gift of the Holy Spirit

Listen closely to the Holy Spirit. . . .
With your heart you'll understand:
It's that feeling that tells you what's
right and true;
It's God's own helping hand.

But the Helper will teach you everything. He will
cause you to remember all the things I told you.
This Helper is the Holy Spirit whom the
Father will send in my name.

JOHN 14:26

• • •

Jesus said to them, . . . "[T]he Holy Spirit will come to
you. Then you will receive power. You will be my
witnesses—in Jerusalem, in all of Judea, in Samaria,
and in every part of the world."

ACTS 1:7–8

And God is the One who makes you and us
strong in Christ. God made us his chosen people.
He put his mark on us to show that we are his.
And he put his Spirit in our hearts to be a
guarantee for all he has promised.

2 CORINTHIANS 1:21–22

Praising God

Sing a song! Clap your hands!
Praise His name! Say it loud!
Thank God for all He's done;
It's sure to make Him proud!

Happy are the people who know how to praise you.
Lord, let them live in the light of your presence.

PSALM 89:15

• • •

"God is the one who saves me.
I trust him. I am not afraid.
The Lord, the Lord, gives me strength and makes me sing.
He has saved me."

ISAIAH 12:2

• • •

I praise the Lord because he does what is right.
I sing praises to the name of the Lord Most High.

PSALM 7:17

I will always sing about the Lord's love.
I will tell of his loyalty from now on.
I will say, "Your love continues forever.
Your loyalty goes on and on like the sky."

PSALM 89:1–2

Obeying Your Parents

A hug, a kiss, a "please," and a "thank you,"
A "yes, ma'am" and a "yes, sir"—
In all these ways you obey God's command
To honor your mother and father.

"Honor your father and your mother. Then you
will live a long time in the land."

EXODUS 20:12

• • •

My son, keep your father's commands.
Don't forget your mother's teaching.
Remember their words forever.
Let it be as if they were tied around your neck.
They will guide you when you walk.
They will guard you while you sleep.
They will speak to you when you are awake.

PROVERBS 6:20—22

Children, obey your parents the way the Lord wants.
This is the right thing to do. The command says,
"Honor your father and mother." This is the first
command that has a promise with it. The promise is:
"Then everything will be well with you, and you will
have a long life on the earth."

EPHESIANS 6:1–3

Being a Good Brother

Even when Sister eats the last brownie
Or when Brother hogs the TV,
Always remember how important it is
To be the brother *God* wants you to be.

A friend loves you all the time.
A brother is always there to help you.

PROVERBS 17:17

• • •

"I give you a new command: Love each other. You must
love each other as I have loved you. All people will know
that you are my followers if you love each other."

JOHN 13:34—35

• • •

Most importantly, love each other deeply. Love has a
way of not looking at others' sins.

1 PETER 4:8

[L]ove each other. Love is what holds you all
together in perfect unity.

COLOSSIANS 3:14

Praying for Your Family

Brothers, sisters, uncles, and aunts,
Grandmas and granddads too—
Say a prayer for all your family,
And thank God for giving them to you!

You will find pleasure in God All-Powerful.
And you will look up to him.
You will pray to him, and he will hear you.
And you will keep your promises to him.

JOB 22:26–27

• • •

"God has heard your prayers. . . . And
God remembers you."

ACTS 10:4

• • •

[T]he Lord is faithful. . . . We pray that the Lord will
lead your hearts into God's love and Christ's patience.

2 THESSALONIANS 3:3, 5

"I will look to the Lord for help.
I will wait for God to save me.
My God will hear me."

MICAH 7:7

Being a Better Friend

Grouchy, selfish, and cutting in line—
What kind of friend will you be?
Caring and sharing, loving and kind—
Sounds like a great friend to me!

"Whoever helps one of these little ones because
they are my followers will truly get his reward.
He will get his reward even if he only gave my
follower a cup of cold water."

MATTHEW 10:42

• • •

"[N]ow I call you friends because I have made known
to you everything I heard from my Father. You did not
choose me; I chose you. And I gave you this work, to
go and produce fruit. I want you to produce fruit
that will last. Then the Father will give you
anything you ask for in my name."

JOHN 15:15–16

Two people are better than one.
They get more done by working together.
If one person falls, the other can help him up.
But it is bad for the person who is alone when he falls.
No one is there to help him.

ECCLESIASTES 4:9—10

Being a Leader—
A Fisher of Men

Who's watching you?
Who's following your lead?
A fisher of men must be
A good man, indeed!

Do everything without complaining or arguing. Then you will be innocent and without anything wrong in you. You will be God's children without fault. But you are living with crooked and mean people all around you. Among them you shine like stars in the dark world.

PHILIPPIANS 2:14—15

. . .

"I am the vine, and you are the branches. If a person remains in me and I remain in him, then he produces much fruit. But without me he can do nothing."

JOHN 15:5

The Lord says, "You are my witnesses.
You are the servant I chose.
I chose you so you would know and believe me.
I chose you so you would understand that I am the true God.
There was no God before me,
and there will be no God after me."

ISAIAH 43:10

Praying for Others

When someone's hurting or being mean,
Take a moment to send up a prayer.
It's God's promise that if you just ask,
His answers will always be there.

First, I tell you to pray for all people. Ask God for the
things people need, and be thankful to him. You
should pray for kings and for all who have authority.
Pray for the leaders so that we can have quiet
and peaceful lives—lives full of worship and
respect for God.

1 TIMOTHY 2:1—2

. . .

Confess your sins to each other and pray for each
other. Do this so that God can heal you. When a
good man prays, great things happen.

JAMES 5:16

"Also, I tell you that if two of you on earth agree about something, then you can pray for it. And the thing you ask for will be done for you by my Father in heaven. This is true because if two or three people come together in my name, I am there with them."

MATTHEW 18:19–20

Serving Others

Open a door; rake a lawn;
Help Papa to stack the wood. . . .
How many ways today can you
Serve others as God says you should?

There might be a poor man among you. He might be
in one of the towns of the land the Lord your God is
giving you. Do not be selfish or greedy toward your
poor brother. But give freely to him. Freely lend
him whatever he needs. . . . The Lord your God will
bless your work and everything you touch.

DEUTERONOMY 15:7–8, 10

• • •

Religion that God the Father accepts is this: caring for
orphans or widows who need help; and keeping
yourself free from the world's evil influence. This is
the kind of religion that God accepts as pure and good.

JAMES 1:27

A brother or sister in Christ might need clothes or might need food. And you say to him, "God be with you! I hope you stay warm and get plenty to eat." You say this, but you do not give that person the things he needs. Unless you help him, your words are worth nothing.

JAMES 2:15–16

Being a Christian

Do your friends know you're a Christian?
Can they tell by what you *do* and *say*?
Shout the Good News! Do what is right!
Be a Christian in every way!

Jesus said to the followers, "Go everywhere in the
world. Tell the Good News to everyone." . . . The
followers went everywhere in the world and told the
Good News to people. And the Lord helped them.

MARK 16:15, 20

• • •

"If anyone stands before other people and says he
believes in me, then I will say that he belongs to me.
I will say this before my Father in heaven."

MATTHEW 10:32

When God makes someone his child, that person does not go on sinning. The new life God gave that person stays in him. So he is not able to go on sinning, because he has become a child of God.

1 JOHN 3:9

Use Your Time Wisely

You were put here for a reason—
There's a job God wants *you* to do!
Use *every* moment of *every* day
To fulfill God's purpose in you!

The lazy person will not get what he wants.
But a hard worker gets everything he wants.

PROVERBS 13:4

• • •

Hard workers will become leaders.

PROVERBS 12:24

• • •

People who live good lives show respect for the Lord.
But those who live evil lives show no respect for him.

PROVERBS 14:2

There is a right time for everything.
Everything on earth has its special season.

ECCLESIASTES 3:1

• • •

Depend on the Lord in whatever you do.
Then your plans will succeed.

PROVERBS 16:3

Please Him

Think about your actions . . .
The things you say and do . . .
Are you pleasing the Lord?
Or are you pleasing you?

"The time is coming when the true worshipers will
worship the Father in spirit and truth. That time is
now here. And these are the kinds of worshipers the
Father wants. God is spirit. Those who worship God
must worship in spirit and truth."

JOHN 4:23–24

• • •

[Y]ou will live the kind of life that honors and pleases
the Lord in every way. You will produce fruit in every
good work and grow in the knowledge of God.

COLOSSIANS 1:10

"Love the Lord your God. Love him with all your heart, all your soul, all your strength, and all your mind." Also, "You must love your neighbor as you love yourself." Jesus said to him, "Your answer is right. Do this and you will have life forever."

LUKE 10:27–28

Learn More about Him

Want a journey full of surprises?
An adventure that never ends?
Search the Bible to learn about God,
Then share His greatness with your friends!

You were bought with the precious blood of the death
of Christ, who was like a pure and perfect lamb. Christ
was chosen before the world was made. But he was
shown to the world in these last times for you. You
believe in God through Christ. God raised Christ
from death and gave him glory. So your faith
and your hope are in God.

1 PETER 1:19—21

* * *

You have been born again. This new life did not come
from something that dies, but from something that
cannot die. You were born again through God's living
message that continues forever.

1 PETER 1:23

So be careful. Do not let those evil people lead you away by the wrong they do. Be careful so that you will not fall from your own strong faith. But grow in the grace and knowledge of our Lord and Savior Jesus Christ. Glory be to him now and forever! Amen.

2 PETER 3:17–18

Stay Strong!

When the load seems too heavy
And the road seems rough and long,
God promises to help you;
He will keep you brave and strong!

The Lord gives strength to those who are tired.
He gives more power to those who are weak.
Even boys become tired and need to rest.
Even young men trip and fall.
But the people who trust the Lord will become strong again.
They will be able to rise up as an eagle in the sky.
They will run without needing rest.
They will walk without becoming tired.

ISAIAH 40:29–31

• • •

"Be strong and brave. Don't be afraid of them.
Don't be frightened. The Lord your God will go
with you. He will not leave you or forget you."

DEUTERONOMY 31:6

But he aims his bow well.
His arms are made strong. . . .
He gets his strength from the Shepherd,
the Rock of Israel.
Your father's God helps you.
God All-Powerful blesses you.

GENESIS 49:24–25

Influence Your World

Let God's love shine bright in all you do,
Like a candle in a big, dark room;
Let others see the Savior's greatness.
Let Him use *you* to shine
through their gloom!

But before people can trust in the Lord for help,
they must believe in him. And before they can believe
in the Lord, they must hear about him. And for them
to hear about the Lord, someone must tell them.
And before someone can go and tell them, he
must be sent. It is written, "How beautiful is the
person who comes to bring good news."

ROMANS 10:14–15

. . .

Lord, teach me what you want me to do.
And I will live by your truth.

PSALM 86:11

You will make his people know that they will be saved.
They will be saved by having their sins forgiven.

LUKE 1:77

• • •

Happy is the person who thinks about the poor.
When trouble comes, the Lord will save him.

PSALM 41:1

Count Your Blessings

I hope you can count really high,
And I hope you can count really far,
'Cause once you start counting
your blessings,
You'll find they outnumber the stars!

Every good action and every perfect gift is from God.
These good gifts come down from the Creator of the
sun, moon, and stars. . . . He wanted us to be the most
important of all the things he made.

JAMES 1:17–18

• • •

God is the One who gives seed to the farmer. And he
gives bread for food. And God will give you all the seed
you need and make it grow. He will make a great harvest
from your goodness. God will make you rich in every
way so that you can always give freely. And your giving
through us will cause many to give thanks to God.

2 CORINTHIANS 9:10–11

Praise be to the God and Father of our Lord Jesus Christ. In Christ, God has given us every spiritual blessing in heaven. In Christ, he chose us before the world was made. In his love he chose us to be his holy people—people without blame before him.

EPHESIANS 1:3–4

Share with Others

What gift can you give?
What talent can you share?
Use your time and talents—
Show God's love everywhere!

Let us hold firmly to the hope that we have confessed.
We can trust God to do what he promised. Let us
think about each other and help each other to
show love and do good deeds.

HEBREWS 10:23–24

• • •

"Give, and you will receive. You will be given much. It
will be poured into your hands—more than you can
hold. You will be given so much that it will spill into
your lap. The way you give to others is the way
God will give to you."

LUKE 6:38

And Christ gave gifts to men—he made some to be apostles, some to be prophets, some to go and tell the Good News, and some to have the work of caring for and teaching God's people. Christ gave those gifts to prepare God's holy people for the work of serving. He gave those gifts to make the body of Christ stronger.

EPHESIANS 4:11–12

Tell the Truth

White lies, fibs, or stretching the truth—
Dishonesty makes God sad.
He wants you to be honest;
Tell the truth and make Him glad.

A light shines in the dark for honest people.
It shines for those who are good and
kind and merciful.

PSALM 112:4

• • •

Lord, who may enter your Holy Tent?
Who may live on your holy mountain?
Only a person who is innocent
and who does what is right.
He must speak the truth from his heart.
He must not tell lies about others.
He must do no wrong to his neighbors.
He must not gossip.

PSALM 15:1–3

Do not lie to each other. You have left your old sinful life and the things you did before. You have begun to live the new life. In your new life you are being made new. You are becoming like the One who made you. This new life brings you the true knowledge of God.

COLOSSIANS 3:9–10

Wear His Armor

Get ready for battle!
Guard against wrong each day.
Use God's holy armor
To keep evil away!

Wear the full armor of God. Wear God's armor so
that you can fight against the devil's evil tricks. . . .
So stand strong, with the belt of truth tied around your
waist. And on your chest wear the protection of right
living. And on your feet wear the Good News of peace
to help you stand strong. And also use the shield of
faith. With that you can stop all the burning arrows of
the Evil One. Accept God's salvation to be your helmet.
And take the sword of the Spirit—that sword is the
teaching of God. Pray in the Spirit at all times. Pray
with all kinds of prayers, and ask for everything you
need. To do this you must always be ready. Never give
up. Always pray for all God's people.

EPHESIANS 6:11, 14—18

"The Lord your God goes with you. He will fight for you against your enemies. And he will save you."

DEUTERONOMY 20:4

• • •

"They will fight against you. But they will not defeat you. This is because I am with you, and I will save you!" says the Lord.

JEREMIAH 1:19

You Don't Feel Important

When you feel you're not good enough,
Remember how GREAT your God is!
He made *everyone* in this world—
You know what that means?! You are *HIS*!

You are young, but do not let anyone treat you as if
you were not important. Be an example to show the
believers how they should live. Show them with your
words, with the way you live, with your love, with your
faith, and with your pure life. . . . Then you will save
yourself and those people who listen to you.

1 TIMOTHY 4:12, 16

• • •

I can do all things through Christ because
he gives me strength.

PHILIPPIANS 4:13

God began doing a good work in you. And he
will continue it until it is finished when Jesus Christ
comes again. I am sure of that.

PHILIPPIANS 1:6

You Find Yourself in Trouble

Let me tell you a secret:
We *all* stumble along the way.
When you mess up, take it to God,
And He will make it okay.

We have troubles all around us, but we are not
defeated. We do not know what to do, but we do not
give up. We are persecuted, but God does not leave us.
We are hurt sometimes, but we are not destroyed.

2 CORINTHIANS 4:8–9

• • •

Now this is what the Lord says, . . . "Don't be afraid,
because I have saved you."

ISAIAH 43:1

The Lord is good.
He gives protection in times of trouble.
He knows who trusts in him.

NAHUM 1:7

You Are Sick

Do you think you'll *never* get better?
Are you icky, sicky, or blue?
Just rest, relax, and remember
God's promise of healing for you.

If one of you is sick, he should call the church's elders.
The elders should pour oil on him in the name of the
Lord and pray for him. And the prayer that is said with
faith will make the sick person well. The Lord will heal
him. And if he has sinned, God will forgive him.

JAMES 5:14—15

• • •

My child, pay attention to my words.
Listen closely to what I say.
Don't ever forget my words.
Keep them deep within your heart.
These words are the secret to life for those who find them.
They bring health to the whole body.

PROVERBS 4:20—22

Lord, heal me, and I will truly be healed.
Save me, and I will truly be saved.
Lord, you are the one I praise.

JEREMIAH 17:14

Nothing Is Going Right

A bicycle wreck, a bad report card—
Nothing is going right!
But even when all around you goes wrong,
Live like a child of the light!

We know that in everything God works for the
good of those who love him.

ROMANS 8:28

. . .

Do not let anyone fool you by telling you things that
are not true. . . . [L]ive like children who belong to
the light. Light brings every kind of goodness,
right living, and truth.

EPHESIANS 5:6, 8–9

The ways of God are without fault.
The Lord's words are pure.
He is a shield to those who trust him.

PSALM 18:30

Growing Up Is Hard

Your pants are too short,
your hair too long,
And you got lost coming home from school.
Growing up is tough—just ask your dad,
And trust in God when others are cruel.

As newborn babies want milk, you should
want the pure and simple teaching. By it you
can grow up and be saved.

1 PETER 2:2

· · ·

Jesus will keep you strong until the end. He will keep
you strong, so that there will be no wrong in you on
the day our Lord Jesus Christ comes again. God is
faithful. He is the One who has called you to share life
with his Son, Jesus Christ our Lord.

1 CORINTHIANS 1:8–9

My friends, do not be surprised at the painful things you are now suffering. These things are testing your faith. So do not think that something strange is happening to you. But you should be happy that you are sharing in Christ's sufferings. You will be happy and full of joy when Christ comes again in glory.

1 PETER 4:12–13

You Need Patience

Waiting for what you want . . .
Wanting while you wait . . .
It's never easy to be patient,
But the rewards are always great!

Let your patience show itself perfectly in what you do.
Then you will be perfect and complete. You will
have everything you need.

JAMES 1:4

• • •

Wait for the Lord's help.
Be strong and brave and wait for the Lord's help.

PSALM 27:14

• • •

The Lord is good to those who put their hope in him.
He is good to those who look to him for help.
It is good to wait quietly for the Lord to save.

LAMENTATIONS 3:25—26

Lord, every morning you hear my voice.
Every morning, I tell you what I need.
And I wait for your answer.

PSALM 5:3

God Needs Boys

God creates boys to fill important roles—
Both young and old, big and small.
Leaders, speakers, and warriors too—
God has a need for them all!

Then I said, "But Lord God, I don't know how to
speak. I am only a boy." But the Lord said to me,
"Don't say, 'I am only a boy.' You must go everywhere
that I send you. You must say everything I tell
you to say. Don't be afraid of anyone, because I am
with you. I will protect you," says the Lord.
Then the Lord reached out with his hand and
touched my mouth. He said to me, "See, I am
putting my words in your mouth. Today I have
put you in charge of nations and kingdoms.
You will pull up and tear down, destroy and
overthrow. You will build up and plant."

JEREMIAH 1:6–10

"I know what I have planned for you," says the Lord. "I have good plans for you. I don't plan to hurt you. I plan to give you hope and a good future."

JEREMIAH 29:11

Using Your Gifts for God

Can you fire a baseball across the plate?
Or rock 'n' roll on the guitar?
God has given YOU special gifts—
Now, go! Find out what they are!

Each of you received a spiritual gift. God has shown
you his grace in giving you different gifts. And you
are like servants who are responsible for using
God's gifts. So be good servants and use your
gifts to serve each other.

1 PETER 4:10

• • •

In all the work you are doing, work the best you can.
Work as if you were working for the Lord, not for
men. Remember that you will receive your reward
from the Lord, which he promised to his people.
You are serving the Lord Christ.

COLOSSIANS 3:23–24

We all have different gifts. Each gift came because of the grace that God gave us.

ROMANS 12:6

Spread the Good News

Tell everyone the Good News!
Tell them the story of Jesus;
Tell of God's Son who came to earth
And gave His own life to save us.

The Good News about God's kingdom will be
preached in all the world, to every nation.

MATTHEW 24:14

• • •

You know that God has sent his message to the
people of Israel. That message is the Good News
that peace has come through Jesus Christ. Jesus
is the Lord of all people!

ACTS 10:36

I am not ashamed of the Good News. It is the power God uses to save everyone who believes—to save the Jews first, and then to save the non-Jews.

ROMANS 1:16

Making Each Day Count

Making the most of this life is how
You can thank the One who gives it.
Today is a day He made just for you—
Now tell me, how will you live it?

Human life is like grass.
We grow like a flower in the field.
After the wind blows, the flower is gone.
There is no sign of where it was.
But the Lord's love for those who fear him
continues forever and ever.

PSALM 103:15–17

. . .

Whoever spends time with wise people
will become wise.
But whoever makes friends with fools will suffer.

PROVERBS 13:20

A person ought to enjoy every day of his life.
This is true no matter how long he lives. . . .
But remember that God will judge you
for everything you do.

ECCLESIASTES 11:8–9

Sharing Your Faith

Our faith is a wonderful gift from God,
A gift that He wants you to share.
At school, at home, on the basketball court—
Spread the Good News everywhere!

He said to them, "There are a great many people to harvest. But there are only a few workers to harvest them. God owns the harvest. Pray to God that he will send more workers to help gather his harvest."

LUKE 10:2

• • •

Let us look only to Jesus. He is the one who began our faith, and he makes our faith perfect.

HEBREWS 12:2

• • •

"So go and make followers of all people in the world. . . . You can be sure that I will be with you always."

MATTHEW 28:19–20

Faith means being sure of the things we hope for.
And faith means knowing that something is real
even if we do not see it.

HEBREWS 11:1

He Is Your Savior

Jesus was born in a lowly manger;
He died and rose from death too. . . .
But the most amazing thing is this:
He chose to do it all for YOU.

He saved us because of his mercy, not because of good
deeds we did to be right with God. He saved us through the
washing that made us new people. He saved us by making us
new through the Holy Spirit. God poured out to us that
Holy Spirit fully through Jesus Christ our Savior.

TITUS 3:5—6

• • •

God makes people right with himself through their faith in
Jesus Christ. This is true for all who believe in Christ,
because all are the same. All people have sinned and are not
good enough for God's glory. People are made right with
God by his grace, which is a free gift. They are made right
with God by being made free from sin through Jesus Christ.

ROMANS 3:22—24

God's mercy is great, and he loved us very much. We were spiritually dead because of the things we did wrong against God. But God gave us new life with Christ. You have been saved by God's grace.

<small>Ephesians 2:4–5</small>

He Is Your Lord

Your Lord is the One you worship;
Your Lord is the One you obey.
Use your life to show others how
Jesus, your Lord, leads the way!

So God raised Christ to the highest place.
God made the name of Christ greater
than every other name.
God wants every knee to bow to Jesus—
everyone in heaven, on earth, and under the earth.
Everyone will say, "Jesus Christ is Lord"
and bring glory to God the Father.

PHILIPPIANS 2:9–11

• • •

If you declare with your mouth, "Jesus is Lord,"
and if you believe in your heart that God raised
Jesus from death, then you will be saved.

ROMANS 10:9

God is strong and can help you not to fall. He can bring you before his glory without any wrong in you and give you great joy. He is the only God. He is the One who saves us. To him be glory, greatness, power, and authority through Jesus Christ our Lord for all time past, now, and forever. Amen.

JUDE 24–25

He Is Your Friend

Always loving and forgiving,
A life with Him that will never end,
He's making a home for you in heaven—
Now that's what I call a Friend!

"Here I am! I stand at the door and knock. If anyone
hears my voice and opens the door, I will come in and
eat with him. And he will eat with me."

REVELATION 3:20

· · ·

Come near to God, and God will come near to you.
You are sinners. So clean sin out of your lives. You are
trying to follow God and the world at the same time.
Make your thinking pure.

JAMES 4:8

"This is my command: Love each other as I have loved you. . . . You are my friends if you do what I command you."

JOHN 15:12, 14

He Is Your Hope

His Word can never change;
His promises are forever true;
So put your hope in His words—
They were written just for you!

God uses my faith in Christ to make me right with
him. All I want is to know Christ and the power of his
rising from death. I want to share in Christ's sufferings
and become like him in his death. If I have those
things, then I have hope that I myself will be
raised from death.

PHILIPPIANS 3:9—11

• • •

So know that the Lord your God is God. He is the
faithful God. He will keep his agreement of love for a
thousand lifetimes. He does this for people who love
him and obey his commands.

DEUTERONOMY 7:9

Praise be to the God and Father of our Lord Jesus Christ. God has great mercy, and because of his mercy he gave us a new life. He gave us a living hope because Jesus Christ rose from death. Now we hope for the blessings God has for his children. These blessings are kept for you in heaven. They cannot be destroyed or be spoiled or lose their beauty.

1 PETER 1:3—4

He Is Your Example

Helpful, kind, and caring,
A humble servant too—
Jesus is your example;
His love can shine through you!

"If one of you wants to become great, then he must serve you like a servant. If one of you wants to become the most important, then he must serve all of you like a slave. In the same way, the Son of Man did not come to be served. He came to serve. The Son of Man came to give his life to save many people."

MARK 10:43–45

• • •

That is what you were called to do. Christ suffered for you. He gave you an example to follow. So you should do as he did. . . . And we are healed because of his wounds.

1 PETER 2:21, 24

Let us look only to Jesus. He is the one who began our faith, and he makes our faith perfect. Jesus suffered death on the cross. But he accepted the shame of the cross as if it were nothing. He did this because of the joy that God put before him. And now he is sitting at the right side of God's throne.

HEBREWS 12:2

He Is Your Protector

Monsters in your closet?
Afraid to make a peep?
Jesus is your Protector—
He watches while you sleep.

You won't need to be afraid when you lie down.
When you lie down your sleep will be peaceful.

PROVERBS 3:24

. . .

I go to bed and sleep in peace.
Lord, only you keep me safe.

PSALM 4:8

. . .

But the Lord is faithful. He will give you strength
and protect you from the Evil One.

2 THESSALONIANS 3:3

But I am close to God, and that is good.
The Lord God is my protection.
I will tell all that you have done.

PSALM 73:28

He Is Your Peace

When the stormy sea was raging
And His friends didn't know what to do,
Jesus calmed the storm for them;
He can also bring peace to you.

We have been made right with God because of our
faith. So we have peace with God through our Lord
Jesus Christ. Through our faith, Christ has brought us
into that blessing of God's grace that we now enjoy.
And we are happy because of the hope we have of
sharing God's glory.

ROMANS 5:1–2

• • •

[T]he God who gives peace will be with you.

PHILIPPIANS 4:9

The God who brings peace will soon defeat Satan
and give you power over him.
The grace of our Lord Jesus be with you.

ROMANS 16:20

He Is Your Joy

He offers love and peace
To every girl and boy—
Give your heart to Jesus,
And He will give you joy.

Your God has given you much joy.

PSALM 45:7

. . .

[T]he Spirit gives love, joy, peace, patience, kindness,
goodness, faithfulness, gentleness, self-control.

GALATIANS 5:22–23

. . .

Happy is the person who fears the Lord.
He loves what the Lord commands.

PSALM 112:1

The important things are living right with God, peace, and joy in the Holy Spirit. Anyone who serves Christ by living this way is pleasing God and will be accepted by other people.

ROMANS 14:17–18

God's Love Never Changes

God's love was, is, and will always be
As it's been throughout the ages—
It is perfect and lasts forever;
God's true love never changes.

God is love. Whoever lives in love lives in God,
and God lives in him.

1 JOHN 4:16

• • •

True love is God's love for us, not our love for God.
God sent his Son to die in our place to take away
our sins. That is how much God loved us. . . .
No one has ever seen God. But if we love each other,
God lives in us.

1 JOHN 4:10–12

[N]othing can separate us from the love God has for us. Not death, not life, not angels, not ruling spirits, nothing now, nothing in the future, no powers, nothing above us, nothing below us, or anything else in the whole world will ever be able to separate us from the love of God that is in Christ Jesus our Lord.

ROMANS 8:38–39

God Will Help You Live for Him

The power to win against the world,
The strength to finish the race—
God promises these things to you
When you accept His gift of grace.

"A thief comes to steal and kill and destroy. But I came
to give life—life in all its fullness."

JOHN 10:10

• • •

One man sinned, and so death ruled all people
because of that one man. But now some people accept
God's full grace and the great gift of being made right
with him. They will surely have true life and rule
through the one man, Jesus Christ.

ROMANS 5:17

Keeping your faith is like running a race. Try as hard as you can to win. Be sure you receive the life that continues forever. You were called to have that life. And you confessed the great truth about Christ in a way that many people heard.

1 TIMOTHY 6:12

God Is in Control

From the mountains to the valleys,
From the desert to the sea,
Our God controls it all, and still
He cares for *you* and *me*.

So God created human beings in his image. In the image of God he created them. He created them male and female. God blessed them and said, "Have many children and grow in number. Fill the earth and be its master. Rule over the fish in the sea and over the birds in the sky. Rule over every living thing that moves on the earth."

GENESIS 1:27–28

· · ·

Those who go to God Most High for safety will be protected by God All-Powerful.

PSALM 91:1

I will pray to the Lord.
And he will answer me from his holy mountain.
I can lie down and go to sleep.
And I will wake up again
because the Lord protects me.
Thousands of enemies may surround me.
But I am not afraid.

PSALM 3:4–6

God Will Answer
Your Prayers

Just like a parent with a child,
God wants to hear your every care;
He promises to answer you
When you take it to Him in prayer.

"And if you ask for anything in my name, I will do it for
you. Then the Father's glory will be shown through the
Son. If you ask me for anything in my name, I will do it."

JOHN 14:13—14

. . .

"Continue to ask, and God will give to you. Continue
to search, and you will find. Continue to knock, and
the door will open for you. Yes, everyone who
continues asking will receive. He who continues
searching will find. And he who continues knocking
will have the door opened for him."

MATTHEW 7:7—8

"So I tell you to ask for things in prayer.
And if you believe that you have received those things,
then they will be yours."

MARK 11:24

God Promises to Save You

Dear child, of all of God's promises,
It's the best one ever made:
When you believe in His Son, Jesus,
God promises you'll be saved.

"For God loved the world so much that he gave his only
Son. God gave his Son so that whoever believes in him
may not be lost, but have eternal life. God did not
send his Son into the world to judge the world guilty,
but to save the world through him."

JOHN 3:16–17

• • •

[Y]ou have been saved by grace because
you believe. You did not save yourselves.
It was a gift from God.

EPHESIANS 2:8

Jesus said to her, "I am the resurrection and the life. He who believes in me will have life even if he dies. And he who lives and believes in me will never die."

JOHN 11:25–26

. . .

God will soon save those who respect him. And his greatness will be seen in our land.

PSALM 85:9